Use my tail for a bookmark!

# What's The Internet?

## Words by Edna Toby & Bob Stevens
## Drawings by Bob Stevens

For Debra, Lori, Michelle
Norma and David

Library of Congress Cataloging-in-Publication Data

Toby, Edna, 1942-
    What's the Internet? / words by Edna Toby & Bob Stevens : drawings
by Bob Stevens.
            p.      cm.
        Includes Index.
        Summary: A simple introduction to the Internet including what's there,
how to navigate, and safety tips for its use.
        ISBN 0-9662813-1-4 (hardcover)
        1. Internet (Computer network)--Juvenile literature.
        [1. Internet (Computer network)]
    I. Stevens, Bob 1948-  .    II. Title.
    TK5105.875.I57T63 1998
    004.67'8--dc21
                                                    98-3245
                                                    CIP
                                                    AC

First published in the United States by
New Traditions Press, Inc.
Post Office Box 1567 Gracie Station
New York City, New York 10028

Printed in Singapore

# What's The Internet?

The **Internet** is an **Electronic City**,
made up of
**Computers** connected to one another.

Before there was an **Internet**, if you wanted to connect **Computers** you had to use special wires called **Cables**.

Can you imagine how difficult it was to hook up a **Computer** in the United States to one in Africa?

Smoke signals and beating drums were early forms of long distance communication.

Scientists needed to find an easier way for their **Computers** to share information.

5

A BIG IDEA WAS BORN!

# Use Telephone Lines To Connect Computers!

Alexander Graham Bell invented the telephone in 1876.

Now anyone with a telephone can join in the fun. Even a youngster.

# It Was Junior's Sixth Birthday...

Mom and Dad gave their son a very special present for his **Computer**. It was wrapped in fancy paper and ribbons.

"What is it?" Junior asked.

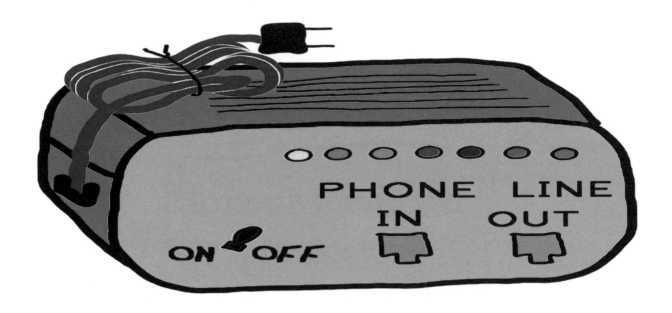

"A Modem," Mom said. "It lets your
Computer talk to other
Computers over the telephone.
That's called going Online."

While Mom connected the **Modem**, and telephone line to his **Computer**, Junior read the cover of the instruction book.

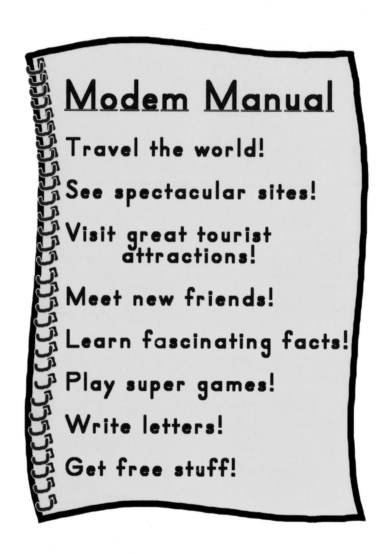

**Modem Manual**

Travel the world!

See spectacular sites!

Visit great tourist attractions!

Meet new friends!

Learn fascinating facts!

Play super games!

Write letters!

Get free stuff!

"Wow! Look at all the stuff we can do."

With the telephone line and **Modem**
connected, Junior turned
on his **Computer**, and was ready
to go **Online**!

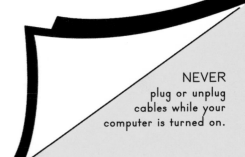

NEVER
plug or unplug
cables while your
computer is turned on.

To explore the **Internet** you need **Browser Software**. **Software** is instructions that teach your **Computer** how to do a particular job. **Browser Software** teaches your **Computer** how to move from place to place on the **Internet**.

Wilbur and Orville Wright made the first airplane flight on Dec. 17, 1903, at Kitty Hawk, North Carolina. The plane flew for 12 seconds and travelled 120 feet.

14

The best places to visit on the Internet are found on the World Wide Web. Use your BROWSER to move around the www.

"I want to visit the Pyramids in Egypt!"

15

http://www.hOme.cOm/

Each place on the **Internet** is called
a **Website**, and every
**Website** has an address called a **URL**.

16

You can find a **Website's URL** using a **Search Engine**.  A **Search Engine** is like a telephone book for the **Internet**.

Egyptian Food - A website about Egyptian cooking.

Egyptian Oasis - See the miracle in the desert.

Egyptian Pyramids - See ancient structures.

Egyptian Queens - Learn about ancient rulers..

The little picture next to the **URL** is called an **Icon**.  Here's the address for the Pyramids...

...and off he went to Egypt.

Egypt's Great Pyramid is 4,500 years old. It took 100,000 workers 20 years to build. It's 450 feet tall. Over the years, the wind has worn away 30 feet from it's top.

Junior learned how the Pyramids were built and looked inside one of them.

"I wish I had a picture of this place."

"**Download** one," Dad said.
"**Downloading** is when
you move things from places on the
**Internet** to your own **Computer**."

Junior had some questions about Egypt and used the **Internet** to write to the Pyramid Keepers. Notes sent over the **Internet** are called **Email**. He ended his letter with a **Smiley**.

#  Smileys

When you speak, the look on your face and the tone of your voice makes what you're saying more understandable.

**Smileys** are little pictures made out of letters and punctuation marks that do this for the notes you write on the **Internet**. Here are some of the best. Can you invent one of your own?

:-)  smile
:-(  frown
{}  hug
;-)  wink
:-0  laughing
:-p  sticking your tongue out

"It's getting late son. Time for bed."

"I want to learn about basketball stars, The Revolutionary War, penguins, trees and building model airplanes, songs that I like, ice cream, the Atlantic Ocean, bikes, clouds, wood, cool games, fishing, French, building a boat, comets and meteors, rocks, volcanoes, making a kite I can fly, football stars, baseball teams, clouds, gravity Nebraska, the Moon, Life on Mars, Oceans, Eskimos, Pilgrims, favorite TV programs and Native Americans, famous quotations, President Abraham Lincoln, puppets, dogs and cats, skycrapers, Grand Cayon, England, and Monkeys, Chuck Wagons, ice, Puerto Rico, Africa, Basketball, World Butterflies and igloos, mining, Elephants, Zoos and Museums, Tours, Movies, Amusment Parks with Roller Coasters, Ferris Wheels, Scarry Rides, Ghosts and Goblins, turkeys, Women, Lions and Tigars, Horses, Quilts, Race Cars, Coal Mining, Model Railroading, Angles, Bicycles, Camping, Rivers, Snakes, Birds, Reptires, gardening, Sharks, Jupiter, Uranis, Mars, bobsleds, books, statues, modeling clay, carpentry, ocean liners, deep sea diving..."

# Other Places To Visit On The Internet

Use **Online** libraries.

Travel to the North Pole.

Play **Online** games.

Dissect a frog.

See beautiful
gardens.

27

# NET SMARTS

The Internet is an Electronic City. Like all big cities, some places are safe and other places are not. There are millions of people online. Always remember not everyone is nice. You can still visit this great place, but you must be careful. Here are some tips to keep you safe.

1. **Never** tell anyone information about you or your family. **No** addresses, **No** last names, and **No** phone numbers.

2. Visiting online can be fun but you don't know who you are really talking to. Boys can pretend they're girls,

girls can pretend they're boys and adults can pretend they're children. You have no way of knowing the truth.

3. **Never** meet anyone in person without Mom or Dad with you.

4. If anything doesn't feel right, tell Mom or Dad about it **FAST!**

5. **Never** buy anything on the Internet. If you see something you want let Mom or Dad send for it.

6. Anyone can write stuff on the Internet. Just because it's written there, that doesn't mean it's true.

## Be Careful.

# Glossary/Index

# NEW TRADITIONS PRESS INC.

P. O. Box 388  Ashland   OH   44805

## "The coolest, smartest stuff you'll find on any kid's bookshelf."

### Phone, Fax Or Mail Your Order Today!

Phone 1.800.247.6553 - Fax 1.419.281.6883

Visit us at www.bookmasters.com

---

**What's A Computer?** How many @19.95? ☐ _____

**What's The Internet?** How many @19.95? ☐ _____

**What's A Computer Program?** How many @19.95? ☐ _____

**Special Deal!!!!** How many @49.95? ☐ _____
Buy all three great books
for the special price of $49.95!

**Shipping & Handling** .................................................... 3.95

Subtotal _____

OH residents add 6% sales tax _____

NY residents add 8¼% sales tax _____

Total _____

Visa ☐  MC ☐  Discovery ☐

_____
name on card

_____    _____
card number                          exp. date

### Photocopy this form and mail or fax your order to us today!